We Bring These Gifts

An Advent Bible Study for Families

By: Jessica McAlister

Introduction

Have you ever reached the end of the Christmas season and felt, "Wow, I missed it. Christmas is over, and I've missed the point."? Maybe you, like me, have had good intentions every year to make Christmas different. Maybe you've intended to teach your kids about the true meaning of Christmas, or encourage them to focus more on giving instead of receiving. But, you get so caught up in the shopping, buying, wrapping, baking, going, going, going, that the whole season passes by and you never stop to focus on what it's all about. I know I've been there. I love Christmas...the lights, the gifts, the time with family, the music, all of it. But, I don't want to miss the meaning of it all while I am wrapped up in the busyness of it. I know that to pass on the true meaning...and the true joy...of Christmas to my children, I am going to have to be intentional about it. So, that is how this Bible Study was born. This study has something planned for each day leading up to Christmas. Sometimes it is a Bible lesson; sometimes it is a family activity. But, I fully believe, that if you complete each day of the study, you will reach the end of the Christmas season feeling changed. I believe that you will see a change in your kids.

This is not the typical Christmas Bible study. I have actually spent very little time focused on the traditional Christmas story. Instead, I focus on what gifts we can give to Jesus--gifts of our devotion, gifts of drawing closer to Him, gifts of caring for those that He cares about. It is my sincere desire that my kids will learn to start being more intentional about their relationship with God and more intentional about caring for others as a result of this study. I pray that this is true for your family as well. I hope at the end of this study, your family and mine will realize that we have a wonderful

God that wants us to know Him and expects us to act like we know Him.

I have included activities in this study that are intended to be practical ways to do what God is asking us to do. I hope you will complete each activity and then continue to do these things even after the Christmas season. I want this to be easy and stress free for you, so please read over the preparation page several days before December 1st so you can get everything in order.

I hope that your family grows through this study. Please visit my blog: http://called2motherhood.blogspot.com to leave me a message about the difference it makes in your life and the life of your family.

Merry Christmas!

Preparing for This Study

This study consists of 25 days beginning on the first of December and lasting until Christmas day. There is a memory verse for each week. Write it down and display it somewhere in your home so you can see it all week. Set aside a time each day to be together as a family. First, read the text for each day. There are verses to read and discuss together. Then, complete each day's activity.

The study is geared toward families with elementary aged children and older. If your children are younger, you can easily modify the study. You can do fewer verses, and have the children draw pictures of what the main point of the lesson is.

On the first night of the study, your family will be studying what Jesus *really* wants for his birthday. As a part of this study, you will be making a stocking or gift box for Jesus. Every day, your family will be doing something from Jesus' Christmas list. Each day when you begin your family Bible study time, remember to make time to write down your gift to Jesus for that day and put it in the stocking or gift box.

Family Night: I organized this study so that once a week you have a family night. This is a night to spend time together, review the week's memory verse (maybe offer a prize to those that can say it), and participate in some of your favorite family traditions. You do not have to do the family night on the night I scheduled it. Feel free to switch it with another night if that works better for your family. I encourage you to look ahead at your schedule and plan ahead for the week so that you are sure to work in family night. This is where memories are made and families are bonded together.

Most of this study can be completed with just your family and your Bible. However, I wanted to do some things to make the ideas presented in this study very concrete. So, there are a few items you may want to prepare ahead of time. Most of these are completely optional, but will greatly enhance this study and make it a memorable time for your family.

Please make note of these dates:

December 1: You will need a simple stocking or gift box that you will use throughout the study and several blank slips of paper or index cards

December 4 & 5: On these dates, we will be making an Ebenezer. I have given several different ways to do this. Please look ahead to these dates, choose the option that works best for your family and prepare accordingly.

December 8: This date includes an optional recipe for Cinnamon Christmas ornaments. You may have another family tradition you would like to do on this date instead. However, if you would like to make the ornaments you will need: 1 c. ground cinnamon, ¼ c. apple sauce, craft glue, ribbon, a straw and Christmas cookie cutters

December 11 & 12: You will need toy catalogs or access to the internet so you can find the prices of the items on your Christmas list. This is also the day we will be shopping for those that live in poverty. I know money can be tight at this time of year, but I encourage you to purchase at least one item for someone else. Some of the catalogs I have listed have items for as low as $4.

December 14: On this date, I have scheduled time for you to serve together with your family. I have listed several options, and you may have ideas of your own. Some of the options require planning ahead of time, and some can be done with very little planning. Please look over the options so you can plan accordingly.

December 15: This date includes an optional candy recipe to make with your family. If you would like to make this recipe, you will need 14 oz. package of caramels, butter, 2 c. chopped pecans, 4 oz. white chocolate chips and 4 oz. semi-sweet chocolate chips

December 22: I have included several different methods for making your own nativity. Look over the ideas and choose the one that best suits your family so you can get the supplies together ahead of time.

December 24: If possible, have communion with your family on this date. You will want to gather the communion elements ahead of time.

You may want to have a journal that you use for this study. Record special memories, things you learn, and insights from your children. It will be a treasured keepsake in years to come.

December 1: What Jesus Wants for his Birthday

Memory Verse: Mark 12:30 "Love the Lord your God with all your heart and with all your soul and with all your mind and with all your strength."

Imagine going to a birthday party where everyone gets presents except the birthday boy or girl. Seems silly, doesn't it? Does it seem a little silly that everyone gets presents at Christmas except Jesus? Now, all the parents in the room understand that parents are crazy about their kids. Honestly, if my kids wanted to celebrate MY birthday by having a big party and giving each other gifts, I don't think I would mind too much. I love my kids. More than anything, I love seeing my kids love on each other. That's a pretty good gift for me. But, I think there are some things that we could do, out of our love for Jesus, which would make a great gift for Jesus. So, what would be on his Christmas list?? Look up these verses with your family and then make a list for Jesus. Display your list somewhere in your home so you can be reminded of it through the Christmas season.

Hosea 6:6

John 13:34-35

John 15:11-12

Mark 12:29-31

Family activity: Make a stocking or gift box for Jesus. Be as elaborate or simple as you want. Remember, we don't want to be stressed out at Christmas time. So, don't overdo it. Use a pre-made stocking or wrap a box and cut a hole in the top. Have several slips of paper available. Between now and Christmas, each person in the family should try to do one thing _each day_ that would be on Jesus' Christmas list. Brainstorm some ideas together. I'll get you started. For example, spend some extra time reading God's word on your own, do a random act of kindness for a teacher or friend at school, clean your sister's room for her, let mom sleep in, donate some toys, etc. Each night at dinner or devotion time, everyone should write their gift on a slip of paper and put it in the stocking or box. You can share them or keep them a secret and read them all on Christmas day. Try to emphasize to the family that you are doing these things out of love for Jesus, not out of a sense of duty. It should be a joyful activity. *Even very young children can do something for Jesus' birthday. Help them complete simple activities. They can draw a picture of what they did, or you can write it for them.

December 2: The Most Important Gift

Memory Verse: Mark 12:30 "Love the Lord your God with all your heart and with all your soul and with all your mind and with all your strength."

We are going to spend the next few days leading up to Christmas learning about what I believe God wants more than anything. In fact, this is the reason we even have Christmas to begin with! It all began in the Garden of Eden. God had spoken the world into existence. He had created Adam and Eve. But, he didn't just leave them on their own. Read Genesis 3:8. What was God doing?

In the Garden, God was with Adam and Eve. They all enjoyed the garden together, until sin. Sin separated us from God. Read Genesis 3:23-24. After man sinned, what did God do?

What was God's plan to save us from our sins? Read Matthew 1:21 for a clue. The name Jesus means, "The LORD saves."

More than anything else, more than good works, good grades, good church attendance or any other "good" thing you can think of, God wants us to know Him. Sometimes we try so hard to be good on our own, but it just does not work that way. You will wear yourself out! First and foremost, we need to know God. Draw close to him, and the rest just falls into place.

I love these verses in Jeremiah. It's like God is saying, "I am here. I am God and I have all the power in the universe. I know the course of your life and I want to be your friend and your Lord!" We would be crazy to turn down such an offer! Look these up, what do they say about knowing God?:

Jeremiah 9:23-24

Jeremiah 17: 7-8

Jeremiah 29:11-14

Jeremiah 33:3

Family activity: Praying God's word is so powerful. And prayer is one of the ways we get to know God. So many times we pray for what we want: "God help this person, bless us, please do this, etc." And there is nothing wrong with coming to God with our needs. But prayer is more than making a list. Use the verses in Jeremiah to write a prayer that your family will come to know God more over the coming days. Pray this prayer every night of this study. Write it and display it in your home between now and Christmas. If you aren't sure how to begin, I'll get you started...feel free to use this, or go out on your own.

Example: "Father, as a family, we want to know you more. Your word says that the only thing worth boasting about in this life is knowing and understanding you. God, please reveal yourself in mighty ways to our family. Speak to our hearts and help us to put our confidence in you. Make us like trees planted by water....(continue, using the other verses to add to your prayer.)

*For very young children, teach them to say a very simple prayer each day asking for help being a better friend to God.

December 3: The Gift of Trust

Memory Verse: Mark 12:30 "Love the Lord your God with all your heart and with all your soul and with all your mind and with all your strength."

Don't forget to say your family prayer! Talk about any ways that you feel like God is revealing himself to you. Maybe a verse that stood out to you during your Bible reading? Maybe a new sense of peace? Sometimes, I walk outside and see a beautiful sunrise or sunset and I can feel God very close. I can sense his love of beauty and creation and his power.

One of the hardest things for people to do is to trust the Lord. We may think we trust him, but as soon as something starts to go differently than we think it should, we start feeling the need to intervene. We come up with all kinds of ways to "help" God out, because we don't trust him. Think about it, if we *really* trusted him, we would live in perfect peace, with no worry or fear, at all times. Wouldn't that be wonderful? We may never fully get there in this life, but we can certainly work on trusting God more. It's all a part of knowing and loving him.

Our problem with trusting God started in the Garden. Read Genesis 3:1-6. Do you see what the "crafty" serpent did there? He planted seeds of mistrust in Eve's mind. "Did God *really* say that?" "You will not surely die." Hmmm…does Satan still do this today? I think so.

Read these verses about God. Jot down why we should trust him beside each verse.

Isaiah 26:3-4 _____

Isaiah 40:20-31 _____

Isaiah 43:1-2 _____

Psalm 91:9-16_____

Did these verses teach you something about God? How could we NOT trust a God like this?

Family activity: Start thinking about ways that God has provided for you, been there for you, proven his trustworthiness in the past. Challenge each family member to think of something before your family time tomorrow. Moms and Dads think of some great stories to share with your kids about your family's legacy of faith. If you can talk to grandparents or other family members and get stories from them that would be great too. Save them to share tomorrow night. ☺ (if you need help getting started...think about times when God protected you, share the story of how God brought you to your spouse, how he gave you healthy children, or how he's provided your home, etc. We are all blessed. God has been so good to all of us.)

December 4 & 5: The Gift of Remembering

Memory Verse: Mark 12:30 "Love the Lord your God with all your heart and with all your soul and with all your mind and with all your strength."

You get two days to do this one. One, because I really want you to spend some time thinking and sharing stories about how God has been there for your family, and two because I know this is a busy time of year, and you may need a little time to catch up.

When I say "Ebenezer," most people probably think of Ebenezer Scrooge from *A Christmas Carol*. But, there is actually an Ebenezer in the Bible.

Read the story in 1 Samuel 7. An Ebenezer was a monument that was erected to remind the Israelites of how God had rescued them. Sometimes we need these visual reminders of how trustworthy God is.

Now, I would like you to share some stories of God's faithfulness. Maybe a time when God protected you (isn't he always protecting us? Even when we don't realize it?). What about a time when God provided for you...everything we have is from his hand. What about a time when he healed you, or kept you from getting sick in the first place? He has been so good to us; I'm sure you can come up with tons of stories. (Young children can simply list what they are thankful for.) Now, I want you to build an Ebenezer to display in your home as a monument to God's trustworthiness. There are several ways to do this. I've listed a few here:

1. Write dates and events on smooth stones. Use all different sizes/colors/shapes of stones. Write with a permanent marker and place them inside a clear jar or vase. Add to them as you think of more stories or experience God's faithfulness.
2. Write dates and events on stones and make a miniature rock garden in a terra cotta dish. You can line the bottom and fill with sand, moss or small gravel and place your stones inside.
3. Write your dates and events on larger rocks and place them in your flower beds outside, or build a monument by stacking them.
4. Build a monument inside with small rocks. You can use hot glue to hold them in place.

Another idea that I love is giving ebenezers as gifts (Christmas gifts, perhaps?). For example, if someone has moved into a new home, write the date and address on a rock and present it to them with a certificate explaining what an Ebenezer is. Or, if someone has had a new baby, give it to them as a reminder of God's faithfulness and generosity.

*This would be a great time to listen to the song, "Come Thou Fount of Every Blessing." I can't write the word "Ebenezer" without singing it, and now your kids will know what it means. ☺

December 6: The Gift of Contentment

Memory Verse: Mark 12:30 "Love the Lord your God with all your heart and with all your soul and with all your mind and with all your strength."

What a great time to talk about contentment! Webster's dictionary defines contentment as "being satisfied." Satisfied means you have enough. You are not longing for more. I don't know about you, but nothing robs me of joy faster than being dissatisfied. Whenever I feel like I need a bigger house, or a better car, nicer clothes, or when I feel like the people in my life should act differently, that's when I get discontent. I hate to hit you with this at Christmastime, when everyone is thinking about what they don't have and would like to get, but we are called to be content--all the time.

Read Matthew 6:25-34

What does Jesus tell us we should not do?

Why not?

If you really think about it, being discontent is a symptom of a larger problem. It is a symptom of not trusting God. Sometimes we don't believe that God truly has our best interests at heart. Sometimes we think he's holding out on us.

Read Philippians 4:12-13

What is the secret to being content?

This is a great truth that we need to get down deep into our hearts. When I was a kid, we called it the ten finger prayer. "I can do all things through Him who strengthens me." Think about that for a minute. The Bible says that when we are believers the power of the same Spirit that raised Christ from the dead lives in us. Isn't that amazing? Is there anything we can't endure or overcome with that kind of power available to us?

Family Activity: Talk about what is making you unsatisfied right now. In a lot of families, money can be tight at Christmas time, and that zaps the joy right out of it. In a lot of families, time is short at Christmas time. There is just so much to do! It sucks the joy and contentment right out of the season. For a lot of us, we have the feeling that if we don't buy or receive the perfect gift, Christmas will be ruined. Talk about these things as a family. In our family, we combat discontentment with thankfulness. I encourage you to make a list of what you are thankful for and hang it where it can be seen. Whenever you start to feel like "there's not enough" of something...not enough time, resources, money, energy, etc., look at your list and add something else you're thankful for. Pray and ask God to show you what your priorities should be during this season. Trust him...He knows what will bring you real joy, and it probably doesn't come from the mall!

December 7: The Gift of Having Enough

Memory Verse: Mark 12:30 "Love the Lord your God with all your heart and with all your soul and with all your mind and with all your strength."

We're still talking about being content today. Satan does not want us to be content. Content people praise God for his many blessings. They trust God. They recognize that "every good and perfect gift is from above." Content people live at peace, knowing that they have everything they need. Content people have entrusted their future to God. They are free of anxiety.

On the flip side, people who are not content are always thinking about the next thing they "need." There is never enough. They worry, and they are stressed out. Frankly, they are just plain grumpy. They are not at peace. They do not trust God to provide their needs or direct their steps. They are trying to do it all in their own power.

Read Matthew 6:19-21

Where should our treasure be?

This world tells you that you need all this stuff and a certain status to be happy and content. But, that is a lie. It is a lie that Satan loves to tell. If he can get you to spend your whole life chasing stuff that is ultimately going to end up in a dumpster somewhere, he will be delighted. The ONLY thing we can do in this life that really matters and that is really going to last, is to live for God.

Read John 4:13

Jesus says everyone who drinks of earthly water will thirst again. In other words, if you're chasing after what this world has to offer it will *never* be enough. But, if you are chasing after what Jesus has to offer, you will be fulfilled and satisfied, and you will have eternal life.

Family Activity: Sometimes our culture makes us feel like we do not have enough. Sometimes we feel like if I can just get this, or if I can just accomplish this then my life will be good. THEN I'll be happy. Take some time as a family to see how incredibly blessed you already are. First, watch this slide show about the world village. It has some amazing statistics. You can find it here:
http://www.miniature-earth.com/

How blessed are we? How much work do we have to do?

Now, find out just how rich you are. Go to this website:
http://www.globalrichlist.com/

So, what did you learn? Are you more blessed than you thought? Say a prayer together as a family. Ask God for forgiveness for not being grateful for all the ways he has blessed you. Thank him for all the ways he provides for your family and ask him to open your eyes to the blessings all around you that we sometimes overlook.

December 8: Family Night

Tonight let's take a break from all the hustle and bustle of the season and spend some time making memories together as a family.
First, who can say their memory verse from this week? Give it a try!

Next, plan an evening together. (or afternoon) I encourage you to make your family a priority. Turn your cell phones and computers off if possible. I've listed some fun activities you can do tonight, but feel free to come up with your own.

Family Night Ideas:

1. Decorate the Christmas tree. Play Christmas music, drink hot chocolate, eat homemade cookies.
2. Watch Christmas movies
3. Make ornaments. Try the recipe for homemade cinnamon ornaments below. You'll make memories, have a keepsake and your tree will smell wonderful!
4. Bake cookies together. Or buy store bought cookies and decorate them.
5. Watch home movies together.

Cinnamon Ornaments:

What you need:

1 c. ground cinnamon

¼ c. applesauce

Craft glue

Christmas cookie cutters

Straw

Thin ribbon

1. Mix together applesauce and cinnamon with a rubber spatula.
2. Add ½ cup craft glue. Mix well.
3. Let stand for 1 hour.
4. Roll out dough to ¼ inch thickness.
5. Cut with cookie cutters
6. Use the straw to cut out a hole at the top for the string
7. Bake at 200 degrees for about 2 hours. Flip about half way through.
8. After they cool they can be decorated with glitter or beads.
9. Put ribbon through the hole and hang on your tree.
10. To store, wrap individually in tissue paper.

December 9: Your Neighbor

Memory Verse: "No one should seek their own good, but the good of others." 1 Corinthians 10:24

Last week, we talked about the importance of loving God and trusting him. This week, we're going a step further. The Bible says if we love God, we will obey him. Lots of people like to talk about loving God, but the proof is in the pudding. If we love him, we will obey him.

Read John 14:21. Who is the one that loves Jesus? What will Jesus do if we love him?

The more obedient we are, the more God will reveal to us.

So, which commandments do we need to obey? It can be overwhelming, right? The Bible is a big book!

Let's go back to Mark 12. Remember our memory verse from last week? Recite verse 30. Now, let's read a little more. What does verse 31 say?

So, if we are looking to obey God, this is a good place to start. First, we are to love Him. Second, we are to love our neighbor. That will be our focus this week. I cannot think of a better birthday gift for Jesus than to love on the people that he loves.

Read Luke 10:27-37. Who is your neighbor?

Your neighbor is anyone you come into contact with. It is your family, your community; it can even be people halfway across the world. As Christ followers, we are to love everyone we come into contact with.

What does the Bible say about love? Read 1 Corinthians 13.

I love verse 8. "Love never fails." Another way to think of it is, "Love is never in vain." Some people seem unlovable. Some situations seem impossible. But love never fails. It is in the Bible, so you can take it to the bank. When you don't know what else to do--*Love*.

Read Romans 13:8-10. What does it say about love?

Family Activity: Using 1 Corinthians 13, make a list of what love is and what it isn't. For example, love is kind. It is not rude. Talk about each item in the context of your own family. How can you be more kind to each other? How can you be less rude? Sometimes, we treat strangers better than our own family. Use these verses this week to start getting in the habit of loving your family well.

December 10: The Gift of Loose Chains

Memory Verse: "No one should seek their own good, but the good of others." 1 Corinthians 10:24

Today, we'll be talking more about loving our neighbor.

Read Isaiah 58:6-12

List some ways that we can love our neighbor.

Remember the global rich list? Or the 100 person village? We are the ones that God has blessed with the means to loosen the chains of injustice and to set the oppressed free.

Look up these verses:

Psalm 82:2-4

Proverbs 21:3

Isaiah 1:17

Psalm 41:1-3

What is God asking of us, as his followers?

Family Activity: Make a list of ways that you can love people this week. It does not have to cost a lot of money. Some examples: Pay for the meal of the person behind you in line at a restaurant, pay for the groceries of the person behind you, make a meal for a family that is struggling and bring it to them as a surprise, leave quarters along with an encouraging card near vending machines, go visit an elderly/lonely relative, leave an anonymous box of goodies on your neighbor's porch, bring your teacher a treat, bake cookies for your mailman, mail or email someone to let them know how much you appreciate them. Young children may want to draw pictures and mail them to grandparents, help you bake cookies or help care for a younger sibling. What else can you think of? Challenge each other to show love to someone every day between now and Christmas.

December 11 & 12: Christmas Shopping

Memory Verse: "No one should seek their own good, but the good of others." 1 Corinthians 10:24

We're going to take a couple of days to do this next activity. If you finish it in one, great! If not, use this as a catch up time. I know I need a lot of catch up time. ☺

This first part is fun. Everyone make a Christmas list. List the top five things you want this year for Christmas. Then, use the Christmas catalog or websites to find the prices of each item you want.

Next, try to list everything you got for Christmas last year. Can you even remember? What was your favorite? Are there things you ended up not even using? Discuss this as a family.

Look up 2 Corinthians 9:7-15

What kind of givers should we be?

Who has supplied everything we have?

When should we be generous?

What are the results of our generosity?

Now, choose one or more of these websites to do a little Christmas shopping for someone else. Look at the prices of what you want. What could that amount of money do for people in poverty? What kind of difference could it make in their lives?

Compassion International Christmas Catalog (has items as inexpensive as $4):

http://www.compassion.com/catalog.htm

World Vision's Catalog (has items as low as $16):

http://www.worldvision.org/content.nsf/pages/give-a-gift-change-a-life?open?open&campaign=1193519&cmp=KNC-1193519&gccode=animals&gclid=CNTP_uH0l7MCFSOnPAodgGwAKw

Sweet Sleep (an organization that provides beds for the world's orphans; has items as low as $8)

http://www.sweetsleep.org/getinvolved/buildabed.html

Samaritan's Purse (has items as low as $4)

https://www.samaritanspurse.org/index.php/Giving/gift_catalog/

Isn't it amazing that we spend so much money on buying things for ourselves...things that we may not even remember next Christmas? The same amount of money can change the lives of people living in poverty. How could we NOT do something? Can you sacrifice $4 to buy a Christmas gift for these families? How about more? Pick out some gifts as a family and order them together. You may even want to have each person in the family choose one item on their list that they are willing to do without so that another family can receive a life changing gift.

We also like to buy gifts from these catalogs in the names of other family members. The family member gets a nice card or an ornament letting them know that someone's life was made just a little better in their honor.

December 13: The Gift of Loving well

Memory Verse: "No one should seek their own good, but the good of others." 1 Corinthians 10:24

So, practically, what does loving your neighbor look like? Look up these verses, and write what they command you to do:

Galatians 5:13-15 _____

Ephesians 4:1-6_____

Ephesians 4:31-32_____

1 John 4:19-21 _____

1 Peter 4:8-9_____

Family activity: Talk about what love looks like. Write a definition for love. Commit to showing this kind of love to each other and to everyone you come in contact with. As a family, choose 3 people that you want to commit to showing the Bible's kind of love for between now and Christmas...and then do it!

December 14: Gifts of Service

Memory Verse: "No one should seek their own good, but the good of others." 1 Corinthians 10:24

Tonight, find some way to serve together as a family. This is a great time to get involved and really put the Word of God into action.

Some ideas to get you started:

*Call the local food bank. A lot of times they need help sorting food and organizing shelves, or unloading trucks. Kids of all ages can help with this.

*Call your church. Your pastors are a wealth of information on good organizations that need help.

*Do you know any single moms? Have their kids over so they can go Christmas shopping, or do something for themselves (or nap!).

*Go to a nursing home and bring cards, or sing Christmas carols.

*As a family, plan and make a special meal for a family that could really use it.

*Call friends and family and ask if they have any coats or blankets they are willing to donate. Go pick them up and deliver them to a shelter.

*Pick an angel off the angel tree and go shopping!

*Bring dinner to an elderly relative that can't get out much anymore.

*Go shopping for goodies and pack a care package to send to military service men and women overseas. (there are a lot of websites that tell you how to do this/what to send)

*Give each family member a set amount of money and take them shopping to pick out a new toy to donate.

December 15: Family Night

Memory Verse: "No one should seek their own good, but the good of others." 1 Corinthians 10:24

Tonight is family night! Who can say their memory verse?

The goal tonight, is to spend some quality time together as a family, relaxing and making memories. You may have your own fun traditions, but these are some that my family loves.

1. Grab a thermos of hot chocolate and head out to look at Christmas lights. Play Christmas music...or better yet, sing Christmas carols in the car. If you want to have a lot of fun, have everyone rewrite Christmas songs with their own words. My family does this, and the songs are so silly that we can hardly sing them without laughing.

2. Make Christmas candy...and then eat it. ☺ I've included one of my favorite recipes.

3. Go caroling. Have fun going to friends' houses and caroling...then see if you can get them to go with you to the next house. See how big of a group you can get and then invite them all over for hot chocolate afterwards.

4. Go see a Christmas play or one of this season's Christmas movies.

Pecan Caramel Clusters

Ingredients:

1 14 oz. package of caramels, unwrapped

2 Tbsp. water

2 Tbsp. butter

2 c. coarsely chopped pecans

4 oz. white chocolate chips

4 oz. semi-sweet chocolate chips

In a microwave safe bowl, combine the caramels, water and butter. Microwave, uncovered, on high for 3-3 ½ minutes, stirring every 30 seconds. Stir in pecans. Drop by tablespoonful onto greased baking sheets. Freeze for 15-20 minutes.

In a microwave safe bowl, combine the chocolate chips. Microwave on high, uncovered, for 1-2 minutes, stirring every 15 seconds. Stir until smooth. Dip caramel clusters in chocolate. Place on wax paper lined baking sheets. Chill until firm.

December 16: Gifts of Salt and Light

Memory Verse: "In the same way, let your light shine before men, that they may see your good deeds and praise your Father in heaven." Matthew 5:16

Sometimes it is good to do a little self-examination. That is what we're going to do today. Read Matthew 5:13-16.

What did Jesus say we are to be?

First, we are to be salt. What does salt do? In Jesus' time, salt was a big deal. Sometimes Roman soldiers were even given salt as part of their salary! Salt is needed by our physical bodies. We cannot live without it. Salt is also a natural antiseptic, it fights germs. Salt has been used for thousands of years as a preservative. It keeps food from rotting. And of course, salt adds flavor. So, as a family, ask yourselves: "Are we being salt?" Are you meeting the physical needs of food, shelter and clothing of those around you? Are you fighting against evil? Do you take a stand against things that are wrong? Are you preserving the good things of God? Do you add flavor to the lives of others? Are you hospitable? Do you bring joy to others?

Talk about ways that you can be salt as individuals and as a family.

Next, Jesus says we are to be light. Think about what it would be like to be in total darkness. I mean total darkness...you can't see anything. After a while, wouldn't you get kind of panicky? In fact, prolonged exposure to total darkness has damaging psychological effects. The world needs light. Now, think about being in that total darkness and then you see a flicker of light. Wouldn't you naturally be drawn to it? Light makes us feel safe. Light enables us to see what is going on around us. Light exposes what is really going on. Ask yourselves, "Are we being light?" Are we a comfort to people? Do we make them feel safe? Do we expose what is true and right?

Family activity: There are so many people that say they are Christians, but you never see it in the way they live. They are forgetting to be salt and light. It takes courage to be salt and light because you have to be different than everyone else. Jesus said, "a city on a hill cannot be hidden." You can't be a hidden Christian! Do people even know you're a Christian? Could they guess by the way you live your life? As a family, think up some ways that you can be salt and light. How can you take care of someone physically? How can you take a stand against evil? How can you be a preservative and preserve the values of God in our culture? How can you bring joy to someone else? How can you make others feel safe? How can you share with others what is true? Be salt and light! "Let your light shine before men that they may see your good deeds and praise your Father in heaven."

December 17: Gifts of Christmas Fruitcake

Memory Verse: "In the same way, let your light shine before men, that they may see your good deeds and praise your Father in heaven." Matthew 5:16

Let's spend some time thinking about why we celebrate Christmas. Because of Christmas, we have been given a great gift. Without Christmas, we would be without hope. We would have no access to God. Because of Christmas, not only do we have the promise of heaven someday, but we also have direct access to the Holy Spirit of God right now. Not only do we have access to it, it actually resides within us!

Read John 14:15:21. What does Jesus say will happen after he leaves the earth?

The Holy Spirit is a power that all believers have access to, but few actually tap into it. Once the Spirit takes up residence in us, we start to change. Remember yesterday when we read that we are to be salt and light? Well, the Holy Spirit is what gives us the power, the energy, and the way to do that. If we are the light bulb, He is the electricity that powers it. We can't do it in our own power, because of our sin nature.

So, what does it look like when we live according to our own sin nature? Read Galatians 5:19-21. What does it look like when we live by the Spirit? Read Galatians 5:22-23.

The Spirit will bring about these good things in us. We simply have to yield our will, or crucify our sinful nature, in order to allow these good fruits to come about.

Read Galatians 6:7-10. Why is it important that we live by the Spirit instead of by our sinful nature?

Family Activity: Talk about what sins on the "sin nature" list that you struggle with. Which fruits of the Spirit do you see the Holy Spirit already developing in you? Say a prayer that God will prune away the fruits of the sinful nature and encourage the fruits of the Spirit.

December 18: Gifts of Faithfulness

Memory Verse: "In the same way, let your light shine before men, that they may see your good deeds and praise your Father in heaven." Matthew 5:16

It is one week until Christmas! In the week leading up to Christmas, we are going to be spending some time in the Christmas story to see what lessons we can learn from it.   Today, we are going to be learning about Zechariah and Elizabeth.

Read their story in Luke 1:5-23 and 57-80

Now, go back and read verse 6. What does it say about Zechariah and Elizabeth?

Zechariah and Elizabeth were not powerful. Zechariah was a priest, but as far as we know, he and his wife had not started any important ministries or missions organizations. They had done nothing that was considered noteworthy by the world. In fact, Elizabeth was barren, which meant she was considered a disgrace at time. But God considered them noteworthy because of their faithfulness. Sometimes we want to do what the world considers grand or successful. But, God wants our faithfulness. He wants us to go about our life faithfully following Him every day. God can take that kind of faith and do great things.

Read verses 16 and 17 again. What was God going to do through Zechariah and Elizabeth's son? Read verses 76-80. What else was prophesied about John?

God did not really *need* Zechariah and Elizabeth to carry out his plan of salvation. He could have chosen anyone. But, because of their faithfulness in all the little things, God chose them to have a part in big things. Sometimes we look for one or two grand and wonderful things that we can do for God, when what we really should do is be faithful in the thousands of little things that we do every day.

Read Colossians 3:23. What does this verse tell us to do?

Family Activity: Have each family member make a list of activities that they take part in every day (or most days). You could include your job, school, dishes, parenting, friendships, etc. Talk about ways that you could do these things "as working for the Lord." Discuss how you can be faithful every day in all the little things you have to do. Commit to being faithful in the little things.

December 19: The Gift of Humility

Memory Verse: "In the same way, let your light shine before men, that they may see your good deeds and praise your Father in heaven." Matthew 5:16

Today, we are going to learn about Jesus' mother, Mary. Read Luke 1:26-56.

What did the angel tell Mary?

Read verse 38. What was Mary's response to the angel? What did she call herself?

When Mary goes to visit Elizabeth, she receives an enthusiastic greeting. Read it one more time in verse 42-45.

Elizabeth calls Mary "blessed among women," and "the mother of the Lord." Mary could have taken credit and been prideful for being chosen for such an awesome task. Instead, how did she respond? To whom did she give the credit? Read her song of praise one more time. (verses 46-55).

What does Mary's song say about the humble? (verses 48 and 52)

Mary was chosen to be the mother of the long awaited Messiah. She was visited by an angel. She could have easily become proud. Instead, she is humble. She responds as a servant. She gives God the credit for the great thing that He was doing through her. She praised Him instead of lifting herself up.

Look up these verses:

Psalm 149:4

Matthew 11:28-30

Matthew 18:2-4

Ephesians 4:2

Titus 3:1-8

What does each of these verses say about humility?

Like Mary, we have been given a great honor. Because of Christ's birth, death on the cross and resurrection, we are able to be called sons and daughters of God. But, like Mary, we should respond to this great privilege with humility. We should not consider ourselves better than anyone else. Like Mary, our response should be praise to God. *"My soul glorifies the Lord and my spirit rejoices in God my Savior, for he has been mindful of the humble state of his servant."*

Family Activity: Discuss what it means to be humble. It does not mean that you do not recognize the gifts that God has given you. It means you praise him for your gifts and recognize that all you have is from His hand. Humble people consider the gifts and the feelings of others in addition to their own. Talk about some ways you can be more humble. (Young children may not understand humility, but you can talk with them about how we can make other people feel special...letting them have the first turn in a game, letting someone else choose the day's snack, complimenting others, etc.)

December 20: The Gift of Sharing the Good News

Memory Verse: "In the same way, let your light shine before men, that they may see your good deeds and praise your Father in heaven." Matthew 5:16

We are continuing in the Christmas story today. Read Luke 2:1-20

Today we are going to focus on the shepherds.

Read verse 15. What did the shepherds do after they had received the angels' message?

Read verses 17 and 18. After finding Jesus in the manger, what did the shepherds do next?

Look up these verses. What does each verse say we should do?

Isaiah 52:7 _____

Matthew 28: 19-20 _____

Romans 10:14-15 _____

The shepherds did not keep this good news to themselves. They spread the word. Remember it is good news. People love good news. We should not be ashamed or afraid to share good news with our loved ones. Some may reject it, and some may reject you because of it. But to the heart that is searching for God, it will be like water in a sun scorched land. Even more importantly, it will be soul saving news. God does not need us to help him save souls, but he allows us to play a role. It is a privilege to share this wonderful news with others. It is also our responsibility. God did not give us this gift so we could keep it to ourselves. Wouldn't it be a beautiful gift to share Jesus with someone this Christmas?

Family Activity: As a family, discuss people that you know that may not know Christ. There may be some people even in your own family. Talk about some loving ways that you could share Jesus with them this Christmas. It does not have to be one conversation, although it can be. It might be just starting to reach out to them, build a relationship, asking them questions to get them talking about matters of faith. Brainstorm some ideas together and commit to start sharing Jesus. Challenge yourselves to share Jesus with at least one person between now and Christmas.

December 21: The Gift of Seeking Him

Memory Verse: "In the same way, let your light shine before men, that they may see your good deeds and praise your Father in heaven." Matthew 5:16

Today, let's read about the magi, or the wise men. Read Matthew 2:1-12.

Not a lot is known about the Magi, but we do know one thing. They traveled thousands of miles searching for Jesus, and when they found him, they worshiped him.

Read verse 10 again. How did the Magi react when they found Jesus?

Read verse 3 again. How did Jerusalem react when they heard about Jesus?

Read Jeremiah 29:13. What does it say about those who seek the Lord?

As Disciples of Christ, we should always be seeking to know Him more. We should always be striving to be more like Him.

Read Philippians 3: 8-7-9. What is the most important thing we can achieve in this life?

Read the following verses. What does each say we should be seeking? What should we NOT be seeking?

Colossians 3:1-4 _____

Matthew 6:33-34 _____

Matthew 7:7-8 _____

Romans 12:1-2 _____

1Timothy 6:10-11 and 17-19_____

*Family Activity: As a family, discuss some ways you can seek what the world has to offer less and seek Christ more. I'll start with an example. I have a bad habit of watching television, or surfing the internet whenever I have some free time. But a lot of times, what I find there leaves me feeling discontent. So, instead, I could read the Bible, say a prayer, listen to worship music or call an encouraging friend. What are some other ideas? Between now and Christmas, find ways that you can choose to seek Jesus more and the world less. If you seek him, you **will** find him, and like the magi, you will be overjoyed!*

December 22: Family Night

Who can say their memory verse?

It is the just a few days before Christmas, so I am sure you have plenty going on for today. I encourage you to take at least a few minutes to spend some quality time with your family. Maybe you could snuggle on the couch and watch a few Christmas cartoons while drinking hot chocolate. Maybe you could go visit a live nativity scene. Can you find all the people we learned about this week? Perhaps you could wrap gifts together and listen to Christmas music. It does not have to be anything big. By this time in the Christmas season, you may just need some time to relax together.

If you would like to do a fun craft that tie into this week's study, have your family make a nativity. Here are some ideas for how to do this:

1. Make a diorama. Use a shoe box. Add straw or moss to the bottom. Paint or color a night sky in the background. Hang a star from the top. Cut out pictures of the nativity figures from Christmas cards, catalogs or use pictures printed from the internet. Put them inside the diorama.

2. Make a stick nativity ornament for your tree. This website has some great instructions and a picture: http://www.daniellesplace.com/html/christmas_page2.html

3. Make a gingerbread nativity instead of a gingerbread house. Cut the gingerbread to make a stable and assemble with royal icing.

Use cookie cutters to make the nativity figures and animals. Decorate with icing and candies. (You can order nativity cookie cutters online).

4. There are lots of free nativity crafts online. I love this one that the kids can color and cut out: http://www.scrapbookscrapbook.com/free-printable-christmas-nativity.html

5. Make a felt board nativity or make nativity puppets. Let your children practice telling the story of Christ's birth. I love this free template: http://www.dltk-holidays.com/xmas/felt/index.htm

December 23: The Gift of Devotion

Memory Verse: For God so loved the world that he gave his one and only Son, that whoever believes in him shall not perish but have eternal life. John 3:16

Have you ever had to wait a really long time for something that you *really* wanted? What did it feel like to wait? What did it feel like when you finally received what you were waiting for?

Before Jesus was born, people had been waiting for hundreds of years for the Messiah. He had been prophesied about in the Old Testament, long before Jesus' birth.

Look up these Old Testament prophesies about Jesus. What do they say about the Messiah?:

Micah 5:2_____

Isaiah 7:14_____

Isaiah 9:6-7_____

Now, read Isaiah 61:1-2. What does it say about the Messiah?
Next, read Luke 4:16-21. What does Jesus say about himself?

Let's go back to the Christmas story. Read Luke 2:21-40.

How does this passage describe Simeon? _____

How does this passage describe Anna?_____

Sometimes it is hard to wait for something that God has promised, especially when that promise takes hundreds of years to be fulfilled.

But Simeon and Anna were devoted to God. They did not give up on waiting for the Messiah. Because of their devotion, God had promised them that they would see the Messiah before they died.

Notice that Mary and Joseph did not make an announcement that Jesus was the Messiah. They simply brought him to the temple, as was the custom for all babies at that time. But, because Simeon and Anna were devoted to God, they recognized Jesus the instant they saw Him.

What were Simeon and Anna's reactions to seeing the baby Jesus? (verses 28-32 and 38).

Like Simeon and Anna, we also need to be devoted followers of Christ. We cannot be distracted by the things of this world.

Read Colossians 2:6-8 and Luke 9:23-27. What do they say about how a devoted Christ follower should live?

Family Activity: Colossians 2:8 says that we should not be taken captive by philosophy which depends on human traditions and the principles of this world. As a family, discuss traditions, beliefs and principles of this world that are popular but contradict the Bible. Discuss how you can remain devoted to Christ even when the world pressures you not to. (For young children, you can talk about doing the right thing even when other people are doing the wrong thing.)

December 24: The Gift of Thankfulness

Memory Verse: For God so loved the world that he gave his one and only Son, that whoever believes in him shall not perish but have eternal life. John 3:16

It's Christmas Eve. I am sure we all have beautiful Christmas Eve traditions that are dear to our hearts. Before we get caught up in the busyness of this day, let's take some time to earnestly ponder the gift of Christmas and what it means for us.

Read these verses and think about what they mean for you and your family.

John 10:22-30 _____

John 10:7-18 _____

John 3:16-21_____

Matthew 11:28-29 _____

Matthew 5:3-12_____

Christmas is so much more than just a baby in a manger. Because of Christmas, we have eternal life. Because of Christmas we are no longer separated from God. Because of Christmas, we have constant access to the Holy Spirit and all of His power.

Family Activity: Pray together to show your gratitude to God for Christmas. Thank him for the gift of his Son and all that it means for us. If possible, take communion together to remember the awesome sacrifice that was made.

December 25: Christmas

Memory Verse: For God so loved the world that he gave his one and only Son, that whoever believes in him shall not perish but have eternal life. John 3:16

Merry Christmas!

 Today is a family day, and the culmination of our advent Bible Study. I hope you have a renewed appreciation for Christmas and a deeper understanding of exactly what it means for us. Here are some suggestions for wrapping up the study:

Get out the stocking or gift box that you made for Jesus at the beginning of this study. Take some time to read through all the things your family has done this Christmas season as a gift to Jesus.

Try to say all of the memory verses.

 Give thanks for the way your lives and the lives of others have been blessed this year.

Read the Christmas story one more time, all the way through. I hope it is even more meaningful to you this year.

 Commit to continue being devoted followers of Christ in the New Year.

Printed in Great Britain
by Amazon.co.uk, Ltd.,
Marston Gate.